# The Morning Came Calling Our Names



*Poems where I reflect on my journey through life.*

John Chinaka Onyeche

World Inkers Printing and Publishing
New York, New York
Dakar, Senegal

Contact publisher's representative Dustin Pickering:
publication.worldinkers@gmail.com

Cover image generated by AI

Cover design by Dustin Pickering

ISBN-13: 978-2-487017-06-1

# The Morning Came Calling Our Names

*Poems where I reflect on my journey through life.*

John Chinaka Onyeche

Many ships have left the bay
And many divers
The water
Knows
Us

This is a collection of poems
Where I will live on
To retell
Some
Of
My
Ordeals

With all your griefs,
Do not die before
Your promised
Land.
*"John Chinaka Onyeche"*

## Blurbs

THE MORNING CAME CALLING OUR NAMES

Have you ever eaten a plate of delicious pains? I mean a plate rich in the heartcries of a burning soul?

If you haven't, then you need to get yourself into the restaurant called John Chinaka Onyeche and let his soul serve you some appetising sadness as a very deeply satisfying food of thought.

Sadness is an unwanted experience by human beings. And if such sadness is cooked with lots of hurts, disappointments, failures and whatever negativity you can think of, then you wouldn't want to touch it with any kind of 'yes!' as a spoon, talk less of feeding happily on it.

But! John here in this beautiful collection serves us sadness in a very delicious and irresistible way. A brilliant chef of words, he takes us deep inside his soul to sit and savour a special kind of bitterness and anguish that is a kind of mirror of man in his society. From him, we eat personal pains that puts us in the eyes of very important questions; that sits us back and look at ourselves and our nation, demanding urgent answers that is a happiest miraculous relief of salvation.

The Morning Came Calling Our Names.......

To do what? To stand in the shoes of John or be a flesh under his skin and feel the throbbing pain and misery that LIFE deals the average man called Nigerian.
It calls our names to feast a special plate of pains. To enjoy it, and at the same time arise with a dear brother to jointly make Nigeria a better place for all.
Thank you, John and The Morning for calling our names out today.

"**Richards Adewale Tanimonure**" 03rd/Nov/2022.

## Acknowledgements

To name but a few of you here

**Nket Godwin**, I am forever grateful.
**Maazi Jaachi Anyatonwu**, I had wanted to name my son after you, but it hasn't failed still.
**Jide Badmus**, how do I thank you for all your help?
**Bibi Ukonu**, you heard a voice in the desert and came out to give a light.
**Chima Ohiahuruagu**, thank you for your support
**Abuchi Onyema**, I have not seen you before but you are my blood at all times.
**Engr Victor Mbanefo,** you are a light bearer.
**Engr Monday,** you are a brother and teacher.
**Jude Thaddeus**, you are a brother.
**Iwunze Oliver**, you are a brother.
**Paul Iwunna**, you are kinsmen from all angles.
**Tares Oburumu**, you breathed life to this work.
**Dr Komi George**, my lecturer, my friend.
**Dr Henry D**, you are a father of knowledge.
**Dr Asiemei**, you can motivate one to read more.
**Dr Michael**, my HOD.
**Alabo Clinton**, you are a book warmer.
**Sunday Wori**, you are a brother.
**Ikechi Samuel Onyeche**, thank you.
**Chidinma Favour Chinedu**, my BH.
**Mummy Magrate Umukoro**, what you don't have you can't give.
**Chiemena Joy**, you are a mother in Israel.
**Oluchi Samuel**, you are a sister inlaw.
**Aunty Chioma Asuonye**, thank you for all your support.
**Mrs Ngozi Ebubedike**, Ma, you are a mother.
**Ifeanyi Asuonye**, thank you for saving the world.
**Uche God-person**, the road we travelled is not in vain.
**Promise Chiadikaobi**, twins as always.
**(The Brothers)**, you are all acknowledged.
**Evans Nwachukwu**, you are a voice too.
**Franklyn Ohia**, you are a brother.
**Ogiegba Alesei**, you have become an elder brother.
**Engr Tochi A**, you are a brother.

The entire **Halogen Guards** working with **MTN Nigeria**, I respect you all.

# Contents

**The morning came calling our names**

& the morning came
calling our names
Children of unloving
fathers of woes
Worshipers of
egotistical charlatan
In the house of their gods:
appetite

Lost in morality
& dignity of characters
Come home;
come, come home.

The morning that came
calling our names
The frosting furrow
of the heavens
Its drizzling dews
turned into waters

The children of howling
pedigree at will
The question posts;
who are you in the rain?

**The holy chalice**

Every morning that breaks my darkness
You are this vast windowpane
The one I stand before it
To glare what a man
I am becoming
Your winds
They
Draw
Me
Into
Loving
You
Unconditionally Just like
the Knight of Saint Lucia
Loved the old Holy chalice

**Dollar**

& our leaders so love the foreign currency, that they sold our naira notes to buy & keep the dollars. But why didn't they consider abolishing naira notes? I mean, our so-called dying naira & take up the dollars. Perhaps, the dollar notes as a way to judge their greed & stupid mind-set of stealing the naira. & why convert the naira notes into dollars at the expense of the people's bread; I mean, the naira that we quest for in the mouth of a pretend dead lion. & at the end of the whole thing, the news reads; he stole 90 billion dollars & I ask; is the dollar our currency & why have a dollar where the naira is your country's currency & why kill it?

**Moving on**

*The deed has been done*
*My spirit is broken*
*He gave me the reason*
*He left me with questions*
*"Asa"*
Last night, I kneeled before an altar
And a voice whispered to my ears
Like the same voice of my mother
On the evening before she broke
our last bucket.

The words she muttered were not
That kind of word that builds up
Instead, they shattered my heart,
Rendering my walls of defence
asunder.

Grief came into the house last night
And straight to my precious mother,
The only thing I treasured more
My family's pride it stole away from me,

The hurricane has left my heart flowing
In threnody, dirge and longing for home
The safe sanctuaries of family bonds
But I have to keep moving on

**Shackles**

And one day we shall all lay stalled in sleep
Like logs of woods in a wooden box unknown

Pronounced dead because there is no air
In our nostrils. Perhaps, if life seizes to exist

Friends will gather to lower us down
Into the darkness, we've once feared of

The body we once beautified with paints
It's now painted with rubbles of the earth

Who knows what happens to our bodies
When they are planted into the graves

As dead and no knowledge of our remains
Stall and stocked within the prisons

The box  with 8 shadows of no mercy
It holds us down till at the master's call

When shall this burden be taken away
From the life of humanity; the shackles of death

## Father's day

For fatherless boys like me,
Those whose life handed a basket

At the bank of river Nile to scoop
Water into their drying out throats

And to what makes them fathers at tender
Knowing what a long walk to manhood it is

They bent on their backs, out-learning grief
Stories once told that a boy is a bag of load

In absence of his father, he becomes a father
And a husband to the hands that nursed him

**Fears of the future**

Just last night, fear escaped from my house
It was through the window this time.

Yesterday, I watched the fears of the unknown,
It crept in through the door I left unlocked

With eyes of yesterday's dream of today
I perspire what garden of threnody that I am

As each day woke me up with uncertainties
My aspiration dancing Fuji songs at nights

In one of my night's dreams, I saw an angel
It handed out to me, a flower with a bird

In another of my dreams, the bird sings
And the flower became a dried-up petals

I became afraid of what I am becoming
My dreams and the longings of my heart

To this moment, I am thinking of my now,
For the tomorrow I am not into it scares me

**The country said**

That we are children of the future
Recited in the stanzas of a national anthem
O, the false bi labial promises made to us
At the altar of national calls, we lied to ourselves
Singing the songs of the delude sojourners
Whereas the unity of this invention lacks truth

We whimper and sauntered towards disunity
Where home promises bullets for another outcry
Just like yesterday, my son pointed to a portrait,
The portrait of a bleeding national flag hoisted
With blood stains on the national unity

And he asked, is this what our country is like?
Where are the promises of the national anthem
Those lines we sing with the hope that it is a promise
The promise made for the born and the unborn child
And were these the stories of our heroes past?

**I am not sure**

If not for grief that I was made to bear
For every drops of the rain I touched
Into a blood they turned, staining my heart.

I once saw a boy, he was clothed in threnody
For the father he had lost at his tender age
And the mother he had come to love now,

But nothing can equal his love for his father,
As each night he would walk into the moon
Looking for his father's disappearing face

**I am parting the ocean**

How tonight I am parting the ocean
Though I have been drowned in it
Perhaps, twice, and my gaze remade
It was not for the pleasure of swimming
Still, the stillness of this ocean welcomes

The children of the world unlearned
Three over one minus four and five
I am not sure if I had the opportunity to learn

Perhaps, not until this night when the call came
Saddle your load to the deck of the ship and sail,
With grief as your captain, sail onto the land
Flowing with threnody, dirge and howling of souls

**Colours**

Black Skin:

And they called me black
The night parted my eyes
Everything evil, they said
I birthed miseries within
I sold kinsmen for gun powder

Brown Skin:

My colour they denied me
My buried diamonds underneath
My blood became the lubricant
My strength they mind to mines

## The returning of the birds

*grief in this country is a pest.*
*It comes & doesn't*
*leave feasting on the happiness of a family,*
*taking off*
*laughter from the mouth of a happy child.*
*"Timothy".*
Each night I remember
my son's away from home,
My tears become my nest -
From where I retire like birds;
Away from the chaos of the -
Day - to reflect on the routes;
Those taken by the cause -
The wind's chosen direction
Fate and the belief of a man
They have not told me what
A broken man - a man can be
Out of this troubled earth
Where a man is considered a loner
In the house of emptiness
He mourns himself -
in the morning rain
And at the noon Sun, he forgets
What manner of man he is
As the evening comes,
He sees life as a bird sees it, -
An empty nest in the returning
Winter days without hopes
Except for that, he makes of it.

**Met wet ice**

On one of the unholy nights of our love
He had walked in and undressed me,
My conscience: and he placed me before his altar
As his ritual, perhaps, before his gods, those -
He calls love, and there I moaned heavenly
Onto the stairways of roses, we walked
Into ecstasy and there the heaven gates
Opened in just a twinkle of an eye

For our love has found its habitat within
The joy of the angels became our duty,
In and out, we regained the lost kingdom
Its Kings and Queens are incarnated within
Our hands binding its fortified boroughs
Until a cry was heard from this kingdom
Met - wet ice, there was a time like this.

**The still voice**

The last time my mother stared into my eyes,
She muttered holy words,
Like those she had always muttered before
the status of Christ Jesus on the Church premises
She knelt before my face and said;

I have seen the brokenness of the world
They are breathing in your eyes
Burning down many orchards of roses
How did this nation become an inferno
Burning out her strength with old fire-woods

When I could not utter a word to her,
She called me the orchard of fire;
Burn yourself and live again like a phoenix
This nation of ours will try to burn you
But I have planted in your body fire proof
You will not die but live after the fire

**Favour**

And so shall you soar upward and say;
To what shall I liken your love -

If it is not like the jar of alabaster oil,
So costly that only the Kings acquire it
So precious that it is not found within the lost city
But within a maiden from my maternal home
She is called; F
A
V
O
U
R
For each night she whispers in the air,
Her love engulfs her man in ecstatic
euphoria
Just like the jar of olive oil pouring un-ending,
That which was gushed out - especially
On the head of God's elect - Aaron
On the eve of his confirmation as a priest,
It runs over and withheld not from flowing

Rivers of equanimity
Upon
tranquillity.

Whispers of angels from the third heavens
There you stood and your love dipped me
In the totality of heaven, you engulfed me
in flames
And your beauty, the first behold of creation
To you, it beheld and whispered;
It is beautiful, my creation and my image
To what shall I liken you with if not love

**Love kills**

Some days
Brokenness
Engulfs me

Up to my
throat, it chokes
And if it prevails

Don't forget,
I am dying
For what it's not.

What I thought
It was a true
Love, perhaps,

A man dies for
At least one
Thing in a lifetime

**The knight queen**

And the knight Queen
Sitting behind the
-throne whispered

Drink from this
Chalice as a knight
While I kneeled

But the man in me
Retorted - drink not
For the cup before you

It doesn't make you a man
Drink not, for there is
No hope of drinking pains

**Farewell**

She came calling me;
an answered prayer

And I called her;
my saviour

And behind the scenes;
we watered our hearts with words

And the gathering of these waters;
we made love of our hand paddling canoes

As across the country and longings
we became one tied together

But the tales of untied tongues continued
we rained eulogies and apologise for the love

Not until last night that the silence was broken
It is over and these waters we crossed

It has dried up and our boats shall be used
to keep us warm in the wintertime

Farewell.

**Home calls**

Soulmate.
Tonight, I am taking you out
To buy you a sip of red wines
From the southern tips
Where dwells stillness.

I know that I have wandered
Away from your palms and
Your love has not let me be
In the middle of the night
It calls out; my lover, come.

Come home and have peace
The fire of your love is going
Down and down it is going
Down and your offspring
They gathered calling you.

Soulmate.
Tonight, I am taking you out
To buy a sip of a red wine
In the old city's garden
Where we once with the brooks
And where the nightingale hoots
Love is peaceful and sacrifice.

**Who we are not**

Children of the day
For how long shall you cry
-in the night ushered in by the city

But yesterday, under your father's hut
Cedars had once grown up and sheltered
The old city houses of the great town

Where is this darkness coming from
At this point, it is not our own
It is not our way before this time

**Never**

Tonight.
As my ritual,
I am standing
Behind my shadow
As it reveals the man
I am.
Not my age experience
I am a man taking many punches
Of my existence as it hits
& heat my pots and pans
I am standing on a pedestal
Where the sign says
Never say never.

**To my son**

Yesterday, I watched my son speaks his first word. It was not until I learned that he has been speaking for the first night before his mother's birthday. I now know what a waste of time and family-bound my work and study had caused me. I remembered the child I have dreamed of becoming his father, and now he did not learn his first words with my name but the names of strangers; those he saw more often than I am. My wishes flew away from the bees tree behind my mother's hut; they flew away with the last hope of my becoming a man and a father to my son. And on this day, grief for the father that I am not to this innocent boy, they have gathered to nail me before a cross beside the two thieves: study and work. These two stole from me, my family-bound with my son who now knows the names of strangers he met on the way than the father he never had a moment to learn his name as he made his first words and pronunciation of letters.

**For Ogechukwu**

& love came, calling me her saviour
But in a return for this name;
I told her that; I am a lost child.
I lost my way to love when I couldn't care enough.

& with her hands crossed over her mouth;
She called me uninhabited land of pains
Where thorns are grown up to scourge,
& to kill the roses underneath the shrubs.

& so, I looked up at the face of this love,
Bruises, the hide and seek of yesterday
They are all visible before every one of her words,
I mean, those she spoke to allure me perhaps.

& So, I now know what a sad happenstance
I am becoming in the house of grief with love
Where my shadow prom with every lyric
Those playing in & outside of my heart & arteries

But who could believe that it once said;
I am her saviour from the beginning of time
In this emptied space called our earth
But in time for this, I am now her death

Where was this saviour in the clothing of a boy
Where was the first word she uttered by
In that which she calls loving you to the end,
Was loving to kill and never being tolerant?
& she said; I have tolerated you enough.

**Muse or me**

To Oge,
Distance has killed our love.

& to Sobe,
Away from home has mired
the son & his father's love.

For the family,
The bond is now let loosened.

& for what is the gain,
Being an extremist in life.

But why never take things seriously,
Perhaps, except for being honest.

**Silent hill**

Tonight again
On this threshold
Of thousands
Thoughts,
She pulled it out
To my hands
They fell in
Threnody like pills

Each day of this,
Knowing her as
A lover or pains
She hands me
Thousand thoughts
To drink and be drowsy
As she whispers
I am loving you

In pain or pleasure
This love is killing me
More than it is life
To the walls of my life
Take and drink it all
It's your ritual pills,
For you deserve it
Love that kills.

## Love called me a saint

Last night, love opened my door
And when I allowed it into my room
It came in and called me a saint.

I dragged love into my bosom
And straight I opened my scares
Those left untreated by ill love

But still, it called me a saint
And I asked love how can a broken boy
One like myself, be called a saint

It said; do not judge yourself
From the standpoint of the wounded
Instead, embrace ink and paper

**Conception**

O, the holy grail
I came tonight kneeling
Before you, like a knight,
As faithful servant
I come to commune
Divinity and creation
To air up my innermost

O, the holy grail
Guardian of the flame
The holy sacrament
The Immaculate one
Come down to hear this;
My country within needs you

My harbour is being attacked
O, the holy grail, come
The purified chalice of the covenant
I am here to drink from you again
For the road is become narrower than
As I thought it would be yesterday

O, the holy grail come, come
I am at the threshold of miseries
Love has beaten me to death
Come with your life fountains
I am thirsty for the living water, come.

**Sermon on the podium**

Last night,
My son told me that;
Nigeria has happened to us.
I asked him how and why
And he pointed out to me
The dilapidated promises
Those they made to us yearly
On their podium, to win elections.

We will build you a new road,
Waters will run through your villages
Your markets shall be ultra-modern
The world will know that you exist
And the school children will be fe-ed

But we demanded an election
And they gave us their re-selection
With guns and men in uniforms
And when we considered a revolution,
But they came preaching a sermon titled;
Restructuring the system of thieves.

**Nameless**

Tonight, I call you my lover
You whose love has engulfed me
Like the flame on the burning bush
Your love has been purifying me,
My pride and the quest to resist you

I am writing to you again tonight,
In the same way, as I did yesterday
With the inks of the eternal roses,
And on the petals of white lilies,
I write your name, my sweet lover

You are the river and still waters
The only place where my soul longs for
To be in the serenity of peace and ease
As your words fertilise my heart,
And given birth to more love to share

With you, I am regaining my loss
Of years ago losses, I have found in you
My lover and my companion for life,
Come with me to the sweet meadows
Where dwells, peaceful streams of love

Come to me, my beloved and mate,
I am here waiting for your ushering in
With your horns crowned queen,
Come to take your place in this heart
It is either you, not another; but you.

**Even though I die now**

I had once run to the hills
It welcomed me with rubbles
I have once run to the valleys
It drenched me with its oasis

A broken lad
A broken man

I run to the name; love
It embraced me with heartbroken
I run to a woman in marriage
She opened her sour and feed me

I looked into the mirror
But all that I could behold,
A broken lad seeking to hold himself -
In a broken mirror, who can fix himself.

**Coins of the same side**

Life is just a reality
Death too is also a reality

How you lived the life matters
How you die doesn't matter;
The closing of the gates of our illusion

The opening of the eyes
To see the beauties of this life

The closing of the eyes
To behold the darkness of the death
From where darkness becomes real

The illusions of sleeping and waking up
They are all disappeared in one; at death -

The darkness takes over the eyes
Who knows,
    perhaps there is light in the darkness

Yesterday a lad behind the wheel of time
He thought about time and space

So inhabited with life, no reflection
And when darkness calls, he seeks lights

At every stage of this journey to darkness
Perhaps, who knows if there is light there

When the gate to the brilliance is closed
Maybe there will be another gate open

One not seen in this lifetime
Lights unimaginable up above there

When today's reality runs away from us
The reality we embrace detaches us

Shall there be a threshold to lay down
Our fears of the world unknown to the eyes

## My death

And when the time shall come
Right before the darkness
I will stare at its face as a soldier,
Unburdened but happy at its embrace.

Happy that it is now happening
At its own right time and day
Perhaps, if only what we wish stands
            A petal of white rose flowers
Placed in my last room rooftop
As my eyes embrace the twilight

Perhaps, read me from the Satanic verses
I am not dying away from the earth
I am becoming a plant in a season
I am becoming the wind for your air
I am becoming the earth for your field
I am becoming one with our witnesses

To watch over your activities
To rejoice in your life here,
To be one amongst the clouds
The wind in the cool of the evening
That is what I am becoming now, I know.

And when the time shall come
Right before the darkness, perhaps,
I will stare at its face unafraid
Because I know what I am becoming
Not something that won't benefit life,
My friend, I am closer to you than you know
I am becoming the reality
The one you have denied yourself;
            my death.

**Sing for me**

Sing for me; a lullaby
Those songs and tales told
In the gathering of stars
And perhaps I may find rest
Within this swollen earth
For some nights are better off - others
At least you could listen to their songs,
the owls' songs
Perhaps, not in their usual songs
But at least you have heard a song
That brings news to the villagers
Are there bitter nights than this,
Where you climb your bed
And your bed whispered dirge,
Avalanches and your heart
Like volcanic eruptions spills fires
And the detritus visible before the eyes
A broken lad, the unforgivable son
They lurk within the tablets of my soul,
Not visible to the eyes that call me
A whole and a holder of dignity
Time and time again, I am lost
In-between home or a strange land
Where to go from here as you leave

# It's a perfect number "33rd"

## Sour songs

Dear Joy,
This is my love for you.
It is love in its entirety
that I give you tonight
On this stratum filled
with petals of red roses
Take it from me, treasure it.

It is from the far north
from where I picked it up
And I travelled epochs here
To bring it to your bosom
Please take it; it's my gift
On this day in our journey

The Moon is up again tonight
But the sadness in your countenance
It has peeled away from the Moon
Its brightness and darkness echoes
It is not the same as you, I know
It is not the same joy I once knew
Come and make your home again

**Names without a reflection**

Sometimes I smile at our arts
Our creativity in art marvels me

Yesterday, the presume mother
Mama ajuru was removed

She was released from her duties
From the entrance of the gates

Where she sits with her baby
A nursing mother and her infant

The symbol we thought it is good
Depicting that this institution is

For those who have sucked well
Their mother's breast milk.

Now, we are left with a logo on
A name without a character in it

There is nothing left to reflect on
As you enter our institution

A name and the certificate thereof
This is what we are now left with

Nothing to help us reflect on
That only those who did suck

Their mother's breast milk well
To behave maturely is allowed

To walk into this great institution
To learn and grow in all things

They are the ones qualified
To be here and gain the certificate

And not a name and a certificate
Still, we want her back to duty

Bring back to her duties
Bring back our mama ajuru

We don't want a certificate
One without a character in it

Bring her back to her duties
Bring her to her position

To keep inspiring the children
To keep inspiring the future

**When the morning comes**

I now know lately what death smells like
As I walked through the shadows of the stars
Through an opening from where life escaped
There, death smells like every sour alkaline
With frosted wind jamming against the wall
All thereof is left to whisper shadows of shade
Unbeknownst that this too, it is an awakening
I breathed last night and it was sour within
The nose is now tasting the sour whirlwind
I did return to break the morning halfway
But, the morning came with fist clung to life,
Since the last night, I had danced with the Moon
To this day, I have been loosening my humanity
Through the words of one, we did profess beloved
At the riverside, where we had watched the seagulls
As they mixed their joy in the riverbed and drank
Who would have believed that to love is to die too
For the first time, love is taking flight into the skies
This flight without a perch on one pole or cage
But many unwanted thresholds it landed on
Voicing the grievances for the aimless flight
Last night when love smashed my heart
It was like a woman who lost her husband
On the eve of their wedding in an attempt thereof,
To save her from drowning in the seas of emotion
There, love drowned him, who is to be loved
There, love immersed him in death
Him who is to be loved, now he is dead

**When I think of it**

& the muse said; I am trying hard
to stop from writing sad poems
Perhaps, those that I die & muffle
In-between its lines, seeking to live -
Again in the next stanzas where to live in
& there it whispers fear & doubts

But each day's events & longings
They kept me gulping dirge into my mouth
& heart the thousands of reasons
To cry & mourn my life & love again, family,
To mourn my earth life as a broken lad
To mourn my chronicles as a sojourner

As the last strength within gasps
It is only left within sounds
I retire to, this bed made of petals
Listen to my soul in broken songs
Those whose lyrics echo
A tremor within my broken heart
How does one grow out of pains
In this world where wishes
Are not birds of roses

## Longings

O! My darling
How do I proclaim you loved

With these thoughts wrangling
Like the ragging of these waters

My emotion run the tarmac lanes
To the apparitions before my eyes

I am in this chamber of doubt
To make this decision to love you

Who knows if I am still myself
For last night love called me Saint

I looked back and told love
I am not innocent of any kind

I told love how I killed a bird
The mocking bird in my mother's

Backyard. It mocked my woes
I am not innocent of its death

**In the morning**

We all have this cross we bear
We all have these rituals we keep

& this & that, it is our ritual
To live a little longer, in this cloak

We see, we stand stronger
To conquer the giants on the gate

Faith is the spring we drink from
I am a survivor, are you too?

We all are demon fighters
Yesterday one whack my doors

To its foundations it whacked
A broken morning with rain

What rooftop am I to hold waters
A broken boot; a broken lad

I am knocking on the door of life
I am an overcomer of this too

The voice of one shuddering
In the wilderness of this room

I am becoming the painted pains
In this room, I am becoming

The howling birds of the air
The voice of the widow of Oz

Whizzing winds wracked me
My abode, my home is torn down

Can someone please whisper hope
To the broken lad and say, it is well

**I am trying to know love**

This is not my usual
This is no love for me
This is not loved for me

For yesterday love died
It died within the jar -
I said it again love is dead

Within the lines of this poem
Death keeps the dying alive
No resurrection at all

What a broken fort I am
Each dawn awakens me
With the thought of
Nothingness -
Who knows what
nothingness looks like

Not until you look at a lad
One with the scars of life
Where love hides and seeks

Whispering emptiness behind
The walls and the jars of the heart

**Love is dead in utopian**

Iyawo mi
I have killed love

I killed love last night
It didn't last long enough

I killed love for it called me Saint
A Saint that I am not

It is a blasphemous one & you know it
It is not in my dice to roll

Am I now a murderer
Tell me if I am one

How can I be called a lover
I mean when loving aches

**I am alive within**

For last night you came home
Perspiring like the summer winds
But your nose blew warmness
And your mouth-mounted wetness
That bridled up the seas within
And in your eyes, I gaze as a pelagic

I sailed to the blue seas in your eyes
They were not the mourning you thought
What you called out was my journey
Into the beyond I fastened my move
Unstoppable the journey took off

I am alive within when you came
When you came with those raging seas
In your eyes, they were tears
The loss of a beloved brother I guess
But I was alive within whispering
Don't shade your tears at my death
I am not dead, but alive within

Kiss me with everything rosy
Place them within my hands and whisper
You are loved not only in death
Kiss me through the petals of the roses
For I know that I am not dead within
I am alive, yes, I know that I am alive again
Within these fields of roses, I am alive

Look within and around you
I am alive, in the seas as a mighty wind
In the forest, I make the leaves clap
Within the cool of the evening, I revisit
I am nostalgic for the wind where you think of home
But it broke my heart last night

That you came calling me dead
While I am still alive within you

**When I saw the man behind a cross**

And they nailed him again on the cross
Calling him -Africa -Africa -Africa
In their quest for plantations abroad
The man became a bearer of a plough
Where arms are better off than kins-men
And Gin thicker than Gene and blood
On the cross of ecclesiastical romance
He became drunk and was nailed down

When I saw the man on the cross
I traced the lines within his veins
And all I could behold was injustice
Those done in the dark watches
No eyes could tell of his origin
Not the browns and the caucasian
All were happy about his nailing
Because it was for their good(s)

A savour of the world they called him not
One who could not save himself
But only gathered the comity of nations
Men; women and humanity at large
They called him BLACK and not a Messiah
Have we not saved the world in its entirety
Has Africa not saved the awakening
The awakening of machines in the world

**My shells off**

& every day
the man within
this cloak keep
growing away
from it, with painted
pains pasted within
I can't breathe
I can't imagine it
I can't believe
I can't wait for it
The dreams to be
Air in the morning
against all odds
in this lifetime
I am becoming
the rubble of
yester years pain
they keep caressing
with avalanches
of the dreams of
a lad on the hill
I am breathing
I am surviving
I am myself
I am an eagle
I am away to
-reappear

## My father and the bees

My Father became weary of life
That he resolved into a wood chopper
In the early days of the harmattan
We would walk with him forty miles away

Into the far East hilltop of the forest
To make fire woods out of the trees
On one of the trees that he wanted
Unbeknownst, there was a bee tent

He broke into their home and we noticed
The stings of the bees weren't easy
But he hides the pains with the cold
Till we returned home from the forest

I had wanted to know why he is mute
But he never talked about the day
The bees and their sting in the forest
And when I insisted to know what happened

He whispered to my ears saying
Son, as a man, you must learn to
Conceal your pain to life within you
As the only way to prove strong

## For Chidinma

My love,
And you have now become my poems.
Permit me to adorn you with words tonight
As nothing again mattered to me except that
You are now like this foyer filled with petals;
Buds of roses, tonight I am here again.
You have become my joy and anchor
In these stormy hurricanes of my life.
I am lost but found within your web
I am lost in the shuffle of the nestles
But I am found by your love stretched out
Just like the petals of the sunflower
I am mesmerised by your love
Your love, I can't deny it, I treasure it
Come home tonight my lover
Come hold me tonight my lover
For each night that I think of you,
My inks flow in black and white.
Come take me to the mountains of love
And make me dwell there everlasting
For your love has found a lost soul
And into the Paradise, it shall lead me to.

**Tales at the gates**

Yesterday, she finally opened it up to me
My grandmother had been a hidden gem
And everyone who knows her did seek her
But her pains she had hidden away from the city
For the death of her only son; my father
This death had left a scare within her bosom

Father died at the mention of a name; Nigeria.
Nigeria had happened to my grandmother
Her only son now lies fallow within the earth
Where his story is about a sound in the wind
And his voice and vigour, these we have forgotten

It happened when everyone else needed him
But not like my grandmother had needed him
Even myself, I had needed him more than any
But this nation has happened to him,

His voice heard at the sound of the morning bell
All echoed emptiness and sorrow at noon
And yesterday, my grandmother opened it up
The place from where the pains of his death hit her

The scars that the death of her only son had left her
She opened it up and told me to hold it till night
Where her sorrow abounded to the heaven's gate
But her tears were not seen or heard by any gods
Even those they promised us that would protect
But in their hands and at their names we're mired

## The forgotten lyrics

And these are the songs of the time
The songs of the forgotten names
Those songs that are not sung with eyes opened
In the cool of the evenings where owls catcall
And over the trees, the Moon giggles

Giggling, giggling at the sounds of our names
Those mentioned in the lines of the songs
Those songs sang for the fallen heroes
Who wouldn't want to be bestowed the name
A hero and heroines of the people

The birds joined the mourning of the morning
As the night has befallen our days
And dreams are tucked away in the wind
As it turns out to be winds of the names
Those we have forgotten in the winter days

Do not forget me; his name became rain
It fell on our rooftop terrace as a water
Wetting the last wrappers of our mother

## My tales

A broken arrow
A useless thing

A broken vessel
A stagnant deep

To one; a sad song
To another; an answered
prayers

To one; an anger
To another; joy

Each day, the gap widened
Each day, the fears disappear

**Moonless night**

How else should I try to save you, love?
You came last night through my door
And throw it wide open and abash.
I tried to rescue you from dying
But every one of your limbs slumped
Into the Moonless night. You called me,
Perhaps, with your last strength;
But it was too late a call to be answered.
For where the darkness had crept in,
The hole thereof, no eyes have seen it,
Daily and slowly you wither away from me, love.
Who would have thought that you will die,
On the altar of grievances and intolerance
Passion for vengeance you nailed on your door
None infers the far extreme you nailed it
Is this your way of showing the claimed cares
Perhaps, nailing compassion for unforgiveness
Love, is this your way to life and its meaning
I know that you have died in my hands
Perhaps, when you could not see the future
I mean, when you have judged me evil,
At everything, I laid my hands on
You have seen the reasons for its unsurviving
It is your dismay that it should be with me
Perhaps, I am not what you want to love
I mean, yes, when you came calling me
Unloveable.

**Portrait of my home**

Home:
Home,
how do I call you
home

When with
terrors
you embrace me

Hands
clung
tightly against my
oesophagus

I can't breathe
I can't breathe
I can't breathe

Home is no longer
home
When all that the home seeks are
To kill
To rob
To hate
To make fireflies plunge into our orchards

## Mesmerised by the morning thought

But I have told my grandmother, saying;
I know that one day I will put off this cloak.
I will die away from her caring hands
They have kept me here for too long,
As life in this body has denied me health.
I now know what threnody I am becoming
To the old woman who has been there for me
For these years of nursing my stay with this body
When on that fateful day we returned
After the doctor told me that I am a day,
I have been wondering what becoming a day is like
I know that the day comes after the night
But if it were death, why didn't he say it once;
John go home and prepare your home
The journey is too far for you to undergo now,
Perhaps, you have but a few days to live
Each coming of the night I desired the day instead
Since I have believed the words of the doctor
I call day time to come quickly but the night,
The night lasted more than the day coming
As the night fondles me with fears of breathing
The day: the day, and the day I am yet to know
Of how it was going to happen to my body
Will the masses throw stones at my graves
Or will they bury me beneath a tree bearing words
Perhaps, I will wait until that day comes

**Muse**

My mother.

When it was night,
She let out her voice

Calling from the port
Where sorrows have

Awash me to trudge in dirge
And she let out her hands

Like the captain lets out
The ship anchor for stillness

Like the sailors lets out
The life jacket to rescue

The man who knows not
The waves of the ocean

And like a man drowning
In the deepest darkness

She whispered to my heart
Hang on, hang on here in

You are the Son of light
While I am drifting away

Drifting into the night's
Nothingness in threnody

Whether to harken to her
This becomes a matter of

Choice of the belief in the light
Or the reality I am awakening to

For the sunrise comes with
Another face of my life trials

Whispering darkness where
I have once been told that;

I am the son of the light
To walk in the light till the end

This ritual of holding to her words,
I am still learning it after all

Who knows, perhaps, if it is true
If it is true that I am a son of the light

## Who is my father

*A poet is the craze-man of the stars*
*A poet is the grand lunatic of hell*
*A poet is a mad-king, a lunatic, the mentally deranged locked*
*Behind the very cold, old wrought iron bars of life*
*(Umar Sidi)*

And the lad grew up with strength
He demanded from his mother
To know who his father was
A question that has left him with
A sleepless night in the streets of life
A question about his father
The teacher has asked him to tell
Who his father was and a fellow student
They make jokes out of the question
Who is your father and not your mother
Because he believed that;
A woman alone can make a child
The lies his mother had told him
To hide away from her pains to love
Perhaps, the lad is now a man
And he wanted to know this man
The man everyone else said that
He looks like his father and nothing more.

Who is my father?
The lad demanded from his mother
Why am I being lied to all these years
Tell me who he is that they say I look like
And the woman as her usual way to tears
She baptised her garments with her tears
Wailing to the rivers that run dry years ago

Calling the love she killed at her tongue altar
He betrayed me and killed our love

He was a poet when I know him first
He was building a castle I was afraid of
To inhabit such a dream was my fears
I became jealous and envied him to death
Even when he was innocent of my accuses
He never minds the ways I rant at him
Not until the day he told me that he regretted
So I chose another way of killing him
I took you away from his home town
I made sure he never sees you again
But each time I look into your eyes,
I know that I am still with him before my eyes
You are not another except your father
I had murdered our love for my anger
I nailed it with chapters from the books of grief
Where the air breathes there are sorrows
Unfulfilled promises and many longing

**Love called off 15/06/2022**

Honestly,
I've had enough sad moments with you.
I need peace for now.
Don't come here to disturb me
or else you won't like the drama.
The beast-like creature I saw on your face
when you slapped me because I shouted for help
because you were choking me
when the baby was just 3 months old,
I can't erase from my heart.
And obviously I can't stay with a beast.
Coupled with what you displayed here
with Ifeamaka and the jug,
I concluded I have missed road indeed.
So, I have decided on how to carry on.

**Dreams 12th 13th August 2022**

I walked with two dead ladies
One is my late elder sister, Tochi
The other lady I couldn't recall
Out of my office, we walked
They had requested I walked them
To the market to buy some things
For they wanted to buy cheap things
Is Nigeria happening even in the graveyard?

Why and who made us humans
Is human the better name for us
What about the other name - man-kind
What if we are called animals
And those who called us homo sapiens
What name can best define us
Do you know what name that could have work
Last night, someone died in my dreams

Where did humans learn their wickedness
Yesterday in my dreams I wept
I wept for the level of our connectedness
One human hit here by circumstances
If you are alive enough
You would feel that human pain
But what happened, I mean,
To this connectedness of humanity

Religion has happened to humanity
Tribes have happened to humanity
My race has happened to humanity
Slavery has happened to humanity
Colonialism has happened to humanity
Imperialism and neo-colonialism
All these have taken away from us
Our Humanity, our connectedness
Our one earth, one body and one life

Last night while I walked with the dead
A third person who took us to a church
I am yet to know who he was but
Into a place where we claim that
The breaking of bread and the chalice
Is for the covenant of the Lord
Where we drank from the same cup
The blood of our Lord Jesus Christ
But we kill each other on our tongues

Is it only in this nation of my birth
I mean, is it only me that this country has happened to
A pastor talking ill of their fellow pastor
Imams speaking ill of their fellow Imams
Members spreading ill of the pastors
And pastors speaking ill of its church members
Even before the very eyes of the dead
And yesterday, in my dreams I wept
I wept for the human that I am but
Is human a better name for us all
Why is humanity happening to us all

A young lady was knocked down last night
In my dreams and I felt the connectedness
With this one, I am broken to the earth
Where did we learn the act of wickedness from
If we are connected this way
What happens when we kill for our religions
What happens when we kill for our race
What happens when we kill for our politics
What happens when we kill for our ego

Last night I saw the dead ladies and before them
Someone was killed in an accident and
Not minding that they were dead too
They went into a corner and wept for the death of another
And their weeping gathered up like a rainstorm
And droplets of these rains ask questions

What names are better off for humans
Should humans as a name better for us

Who gave us this name and why
Because when we forget our connectedness
And the little breathe that gasps our noses
And when we kill in our tongues and tools
Where are we keeping this connectedness at

Last night in my dreams someone was killed
It was an accident that she died of but
Everyone living and the dead too cried for her
And when I woke up, I pondered why
Why do we humans in this world kill ourselves
For reasons that are not connected enough
For religion, politics or the otherwise
But one thing is that we have forgotten
Before religion, we are humans
Before politics, we have been humans
Before race and tribe, we are humans
And let humanity define us all

**10/08/2022**

Each passing of the day
My heart bleeds unending
The shadows I once called love
They all have a rotten bread
Underneath their cobwebs

Those they laced around me
Calling me love and their lover
All of this amount to nothing
But the illusion of hiding and seek
Using my emotions to play dice
At the altar of lust and not love

For what is love when it hides grief
For what is love when it hides lust
For what is love when it comes to kill
For what is love when you hide behind it

Jumping over the fence of trusts
Hiding under the shades of selfishness
Calling out to love and in disguise
I love you, I love, I love you
Until the bird died in your hands
Because you have called it love
While it was choking it up

**I am writing a poem again**

My editor called last night
He asked me what I was doing
I told him that I am writing again
And said for what reason;
I told him that I would like to breathe
Last night, I wrote a poem about myself
In the stanzas of this poem,
I am not inhaling and exhaling
I was stalled and stocked within its lines
This poem, tells of my tales and
It has stocked within my throat - coals,
Coals with live embers that burn me
Not to death even more not to death,
I am in-between its lines like a deer
In the winter rain stocked with two trees
In this poem, I have struggled to find life,
But all it embraced me with is that I am not
Perhaps death in this line of this metaphor
That a boy's tale is the tale of the winter wind
It blows when he less expected them
They came clenching him down to the earth
From where everything about him is like a sand
Washed by the stormy wind of the winter days

**When the storm came**

How I wish you had known this,
That last night, I painted you as a goddess
Within the walls of my heart a perfect god
To worship at your altar in silence, perhaps,
As a maiden of honour to my crown.

But it was not until the stormy winds came
Out from your mouth as words came
And washed off the traces of this lacquer
The pictures of our love together
In this little winter shelter,

When the storms came,
They shattered the haven of our love
On this altar where we once worshipped
The golden images of togetherness
The words you spilt in anger
They watered down the portraits

## Gold

In the darkest
part of this room,
there is a silhouette
from where the spark
enters us to ignite

In pain, I am an elixir
In the furnace, I am
The iron turns into
Gold. for the alchemist
I burn into a fine gold

To the downtrodden
I am the jewels and
They seek after me - gold
In the hands of the rich
And in the hands of the
Poor, I am not changed

## First night with rain

It's a blue Friday
The heavens
Rained blue hails &
Dew over me

I am becoming
The space
After the downpour
I hope to cloud again

## Let's go fishing

And the battle is over
Victory to one who stood
Strong and lasting
Not without bruises
Painted pains pasted
All are the battle fought
Against this year, and
Let's go to the fishing pond
Who knows what awaits us
A big Atabala fish perhaps

## Fisherman

Let's go fishing
My words shall be
Like the season of fish
And my metaphors
As the hooks laid down
My story as the rivers
From where my metaphors
Shall fall into the deep
And catch for me -fishes

The reasons to live on
My life as a fisherman
In this way, I will hold on
After this stormy wind,
I will relaunch my hooks
For I know, there is a fish
Beneath every river
For all the fishermen

**Someday, I will breathe water**

Am I now an image of a boy before a river?
Naked and staring at the altar of the gods
Plotting a graph on how to escape from life
The life he had dreamed of becoming
They all have grown wings and dashed out
Into the land of no returns as a whirlwind

It is said that dreams come true
But yesterday a boy baptised himself
With waters ranging from his eyes
Plummeting into the deepest paths of the sea
After withholding himself from sailing the ship
Because he stayed at the bay for too long

He had learned how divers save the lost in the water
So he had also learned how not to dive into the sea
And to be saved by any diver too
Except to be rescued lifeless from the sea
For this craft, he is becoming a champion
A master of grief and threnodies
Trans-versing this pond called body

It was not a dream anymore this time
Perhaps, someday, I will breathe water
As a boy, he ripens with many dreams and desires
To become a part of these creations
He delves into many promising things
But all are plummeting within the seas of failure

But last night, the boy decided to find peace
Within the bodies of water that he had watched from its banks
There he planted his body to be amongst the reeds
Perhaps, at least to wave hands to dreams
Those that never come true - through planting
One's body into the sea to be at peace

**Atonement**

Rain,
Rain if you know
what a broken roof
I inhabit

Rain:
Rain, you shouldn't
have come with the wind
to render me homeless

On this gloomy day,
I am drenched in every
splashing of waters
from on high

Is it possibly a blessing
or I build my castles
in the way of the wind

## Sometime, I feel lonely too

And I start to pour words on
My grief and their feelings
When the room becomes tilt
Where my world are now words
I mean, I have been locked up here
Together with the gods and I conversed
In every stanza that I have written
I see them flapping their wings
Oh, brown skin gods flapping
Their wings hold me from falling
Falling into this abyss of loneliness
Pages of paper are not enough
Enough to pour down my heart
Which is cloudy with many drops of rain
I mean, in the other of my lonely days,
I have to admit that now I am
Becoming like the gods in here

**Stillbirth**

When the tears rolled down last night
It was not for the joy of motherhood
It was not for the brilliance of the sun
It was a stillbirth of many dreams

The joy and journey through cut short
The death of the reeds at the river bank
When the visitors visited the river
They find it empty and unsatisfactory

The cutting off of the reed flowers
The mistake of yesteryear still hurts
If it is not forgiven and forgotten
We will all die in the heart and hands

# Call it 33rd Perfectly

**Tales not told**

On the night love betrayed us
At the river bank of our voyage
Even the reeds know our stories

The stories of a promised heaven
Across the tears formed by our howls
And there our kinsmen exchanged us

With the same voices of chants
With the same love, we agreed
To onboard the ships to misery

Where our humanity is ripped off
Our skins inhabited whipping
Our souls became neighbours to hell

Who would have thought us a wastage
Where we had once been warriors
If not at the altar of brotherly greed

Are we not more numbered than they
Those who anchored by the waterfront
Buying and selling their shrewdness

We are culprits of these things too
Are we not the hands that armed them
When are we going to take responsibility

**Confession 1**

I call you love
Because from the first day
You have shown me
nothing but love

In anger you loved
In peace, you loved too
And neutrality
You are nothing but love

**You are my heaven**
*Dedicated to Chidinma*

You are loved
For each night
That I think of it
Loving You More
They become steps
To walk me into the orbit
Their presumed heaven
But no.
There is no heaven
Heaven is only an allegory find
Within the heart of lovers
To which we are one
Perhaps for the stars
Yes, we have them up there
But I am looking into your eyes tonight
And the stars therein
They whisper eternity
To this love so pure
Hold on to it, and
Till the morning comes
Know that you are my heaven
Where I will forever find peace
Dwell in your shades of love

**Resonance**

I know that
I am not dying now
But yesterday
a man desired to die
And he died and
they buried him
for three days

On the first day,
they killed a cow
And on the second day,
they wake and keeping

On the third day,
they brought him back
And made it look like
we celebrate death
And turns our backs to life

They bought him a dome
Perhaps to house the earth
Repainted and repaired
His licking hut of yesteryears

Shame: shame on us
When we live in the dirt in life
And live in cleanliness in death
Where it profits us not
And making death desirable
Perhaps our lives a miserable

## Night, her rituals

And again tonight,
The bridge is cut off

At the sound of the dreams
Walking majestically
To the shadows of reality

Its tremor loosened the dots that hold(s)
And into the seabed
The last hope sinks

Do not come calling me
An unbeliever, perhaps,
I had once believed in miracles

The gods and the tales
Of becoming a man
This craft of bearing falsehood

I have comforted myself with many nights
The preacher once told me that;

As a man, you will need to work your life out
For that is your calling in this sphere

Then I went about seeking what it was
that makes me the man I long to be

## As if nights are not for rituals

Just as the bells ring tonight again
I have come to worship you again
I have come to worship my grief
As they all congregated tonight
In this altar of nothingness
Where the shadows of failure lurk

The thousand thoughts in my head
The one dream I have had
The bridges crossed so far
The emptiness that still looms
The boy child that is a threnody

I have walked 360 degrees
For this worship not to hold tonight
But I don't have the courage not to mourn
If mourning could save me on this altar
Let me mourn till my salvation comes

I am becoming an ocean drowning itself
The little fishes within me said that I am sour
Tonight, they have all left my abode
And even life outside the water is not safe
But they are dying for the peace they seek

How do you tell a fish to live outside the water
And a child not suck its mother's mike
Perhaps, a man to not love his family
And woman to live her home for another
Perhaps, this is not the time for this worship

Put up the ritual light and call out the spirits
Kneel before them and ask for your forgiveness
If they know what a broken fort you are
Perhaps, they may find it somewhere or within
There where the light of pains enters your heart
To seal you away from the pains of this life

**This is not Nigeria**

Yesterday as I lay down on my couch
The gentle wind carers my body
And I transcended to another sphere

There was a smile on my face
Wiggling and giggling I screamed
As a voice whispered to my ears

Wake up it is not in Nigeria
Wake up you are just dreaming
Wake up ASUU is still on strike

Yesterday as I lay down my body
To find peace within the stillness
And to dream of new dreams

I saw the police caring for the masses
The armies kissing peace on her head
The politicians fulfilling their promises

But I heard another voice saying
Wake up: wake up, wake up my child
This is not your Nigeria but a dream

**You are your salvation**

It was becoming a murky day
When she reached out her hands
To the last yam in the house
She diced it in the shape of a Moon
Wiggling, she said that they were light
Because we have read from the book
Those where our tales were told unwise
In metaphors and allegories to our falls
Because they feared our knowledge
If they know that they are the saviour
The salvation of the human race
We may go into extinction of the earth
This misjudgement has now lasted aloft
But tonight, my mother whispered to me
You are the salvation that you seek in a man
That man hanging on the cross you stared at
That is your forerunners you see so
They were used to build a city but city-less
What else do desire to know of yourself
If not that you are told that there was a tale
A woman who is left with a jar of oil
And she could not multiply her oil
To light up the darkness within her abode
But has lived mourning the same debt
The same death that took her husband
It lies within the last tuba of yam
Waiting for it to be eaten and they die off
But not again, she whispered to my ears
Care for today and tomorrow will care of itself
Don't forget to live today and leave tomorrow
It is already occupied by its troubles
How do men have light in their palms
And in darkness, they roamed seeking for it
Look within you and see what you seek
They lied to you about the salvation outside you

**Shooting star**

And she touched my torso
And said that; I am now her
Shooting star. My woman
My everything in-between
Each night she would bend
Listening to the night crickets
And in our compound, we sat
She points at the shining stars

And said; one day at a time
You will become like them,
To give light to your night
In this dark world, we live in
All these words she whispers
They became the firmament
From where my stars anchored
Daily they grow to glow my night

And the dreams that I chase,
They are now growing wings
Just like an Eagle bird they fly
But my grandmother's words
They keep me afloat above,
The skies and all the flying dreams
As I am now caressing one,
Perhaps it will live to tell of me

**And this love is expressing itself**

Rain on me, sweet names
What else is more loving
If it is not woven into expressing
With-it sweet naming

Tonight, I will be outside again
On this cold night of our outing
While we watch the Moon dance
The stars and the firmament spin

I will lay down my ears and heart
To hear you baptise my being with names
Those that are welcoming-
The lost souls to a kingdom of love

**Love that is cleans**

As the last light lite off
My lover whispered to me;
Baptize me, my love
As an act of revisiting love.

In this ocean of your love for
Don't fail to dip me slowly
Slowly, until I am saturated
With this love like water

Dip me underneath
Where I shall be declared
One amongst the chosen
By the master of love

Dip me slowly until I am clean,
Dip me into your well of love
Slowly until I am declared loved
Dip me until lust scars are wiped off

**Freedom**

Free world.
Sometimes I am lost
In between this word
Free world.

How free indeed is our world
Yesterday a man was killed
They called him an unbeliever
And I ask how free are we.

Free Speech
My father called me words,
And he never spoke one
And each night he would adorn me
With silence and never speak

Am I not better-called Silence
Perhaps he should be speaking
Or he should have called space
Where everything is inhabited
Where indeed is our freedom

**Seeking peace**

And the Moon danced
In the face of the river omoba
As the land was troubled
The dancing of the water
They called it seethes

But I returned to the threshold
With choices lying before me
I am chosen joy over sadness
I am chosen love over hatred
I am chosen peace over chaos

Look into the troubled water
What do you see before you
The portrait of a boy raining storms
Look into the troubled water
You will see the shadow of a boy
Dancing with the wind of life

**In-between**

Happiness and I have been friends
But not until last night
Not until last night
That happiness unsheathe
A machete of betrayal
Cutting me into a thousand
Piece unrecognisable
On the altar of guile

Now, how do I sing this song
The songs of the betrayed one
Sing within the shades of the heart
Where dwells swells of shards
Of heart and soul of a wanderer

Now, I am singing to my mountain
Perhaps, my valley will not be denser

**Travelling to home**

In this cathedral of hallowedness
We all gathered tonight again
We gathered to mourn home
A country in disarray
Where we find wholes
In the pocket of our leaders
The animal kingdom
Where baboons swallow educational funds
To live in the forest of our parliament

Yesterday, I awaken to a new name
The angel who called me by the name said,
You must run to the hills of the land
Announcing salvation in disintegration
Force none to the cross of this torture
Let everyone wake at their own time
Salvation or none at the end of the home
We will live to the retelling of our stories

**About last night**

Let me hold your hands tonight
Let me walk you home again
In this garden full of roses and daffodils
Each opening its petals to the Sunray
Should loving you not be as such?

I have waited for this moment
When each passing night
I became an astronomy
Watching the movement of stars
But tonight, you are the star
And I am here watching you

Should loving you not shine as the stars
And the openness of our hearts
Like the daffodils and budding roses
Along the rivers of stillness
Does loving you have a colour?
Oh, come and quench this taste
Give me your hands and let's walk
Into this love, let our stars shine

**In my country**

And last night
Our butterfly
Flew away
Not from our
hands but
From our
Scars

**My country**

Oh,
How this contraction
Keep taken away from us
Our humanity
Our sanity
We keep going insane
Everyone wants to exploit
Another can even kill
Is this what it means
To be a nation?

**New name**

I once held water
In my head
And I swim
To the shore
And the ocean
Held its fist
Against my throat

Am I becoming a fish
Or is it just my emotions
Trying to sail away from
My grief?

Just call me the things
Those living under the
Water.

**Shades**

I am working
tirelessly
to hinge
the edge
from where
Grief escaped

Look within here
Have you seen
The hole
They are hidden
Behind my words

**How do you save a man from his grief**

And yesterday
a man-made water
with his grief
large enough to hold
his ship and its sailing

And from my windows
I had watched him
to submerged
into his thoughts

I am not a diver today
perhaps to have rescued him
from his thousand agonies
but I am just a wordsmith
hiding my griefs in metaphors

Do our words save the dying
one who has drowned himself
perhaps, or herself in the ocean
of a thousand thoughts

How tremor besieges us
from the broken edges
of our long dwells in ill thoughts
where we see no reason again
to live this life as a gift

A little thinking about now
and leaving tomorrow its own
for it shall take care of itself
enjoy the now in cheerfulness

stop desiring to die now
while there is a place called
tomorrow for only the living
who endures their now

**Our country's prayer**

Our fathers
Who at in Aso-Rock
May shallow remain in your brains
And may you never happen to us again

In 2023, may we vote you all out
With our one vote and voice
May we redeem ourselves
From your backwardness

And as we have lost many in your hands
So may the INEC help us to regain our mandate
To transmit our good results
Throughout all the pulling units

So help us to go get your PVC today
Because your vote must count in 2023
Nigeria is our country and 2023 is the year
To show that no other year remains
This we ask throughout the nation

Amen.

## Today’s news

and the ship
that we have
waited for has
arrived at the bay

but with griefs
loaded and failed
promises made
on the podium
of our national
discuss and dine

tongue of lies
eyes of deceit
words of the wind
wrecking harbours
where we once
gathered for peace

who had believed
that the change
we chanted yesterday
would become
our miseries of
today's news

## The morning came with shards

And the morning comes
From where it hung in the twilight
Calling us children of a thousand howls
Across the rivers of grief and dirge
Where our voices are muffled
In pretence and unspoken grieves
Because our fathers had promised
They promised us on the podium
That if we cast our votes, perhaps
These promises are to be fulfilled
In the cool of the day before the sunset
We are running looking for shades
Away from the centre that had held us
Children of a thousand howls
How do you cry over your crown
Is it now unfitted, perhaps,
We have survived the season
Of draught and pestilence
And the fattening season is here
Cast your votes on the fertile ground
For the gods have heard your cries

**Wing being**

I have returned
to this rubble
-called home.

I have watched the world
through the window of time,
But the day keeps
-growing wings.

And my dreams,
They are taking a thought
To fly away from my hands

Perhaps, like the birds.
Perhaps they are trying
to master the arts of flying.

But am I now a wing being
Perhaps, I am still a man;

And if this bird flies away,
Would it still come back
To nest its way to the end?

## Poetry 1

I am excavating
Traumas out of me
It may take time to
Discover the Treasure
Those buried beneath
The surface of my existence
Perhaps, salvation lies in lines
Those not deciphered today
So, let us ride to the other side
Of these pains, there may be
A Saviour, one we may have forgotten

**Fish and nets**

On the eve of our sail
On this shoreline
We had wanted a safe sailing
But the winds of emotions came
Renting our havens
And we parted away from each other
For nothing else could be said
That this sea is ranging
Yes, it is wracking our hearts
With shadows of grief and hatred
What had begun in peace and now
It is a place where we murder our lives
Loving yesterday than today in our hands

How do you tell what weather is best
To cast your nets and for a catchy
The lost fishes of the ocean drift by love
To be caged for the freedom it sees in a net
Anchorage eluded the fish over the nets
This is the same way ill love cages us

**Nights**

As I make my bed in your arms again tonight,
Allow me to baptised you
With my words of sapphire
Sharpening your edges
With wet melodies of my tongue
In this island of watering feeling
Perhaps, what is better for one's lover
Perhaps, if not to praise one's love
As I am drawn and I am drowning
In this ocean of your lovely hands
This love is flowing and flowering
Earth as a garden where we plant words
Of love as a flower to help us breathe
In their oxygen and survive

**Poetry 2**

I am inside a shell
Trying to find my way
Out of my griefs

Read this again
and don't forget
I have been here
for a while now

Poetry is sadness
Poetry is madness
Trying to escape
And demonstrated

In languages and
Metaphors in the
pages of papers

### The praying part of my life

Oh, Lord, hear my prayers.
I kneeled here with my grief before thee
My tongue is tied behind the cider of grief
And under my knees are thorns choking

Away from me, the little life I have desired
To live and be found in the dreams I carry
Within the eyes of my heart and my soul

Dear Lord, I am breathing the sulfur within
Where I had wanted to breathe life and air
There this life has shown me only escape

Routes to usher me into terrain I don't know
And time is running with the formula one car
I looked into the mirror and all I see is shards

This is a piece of a boy, the one I am yet
To hold me up just as bowls hold water

**Poetry 3**

Each coming of the night
I have sat watching the Moon
Unshelling itself from the darkness
Just like my griefs unshelled itself within
And leaving in my hands; wings
To fly into the world of thoughts
Where I am pushing to the edge
Everything that has held me down

Yesterday a poet said poetry is life
I smiled and asked what he meant
He ploughed a graph showing grief
The hearts throbbing through storms
And said; this is how poetry is life
Since he finds himself saving himself
Through every thought, he wrote out
And there he still finds his emptiness
They lay there and whisper wings
Those as a poet that he had flown on

I told him that I am not a poet today
That poetry saves as he had told me
But I told him that poetry is a death too
I ploughed another graph and gave it to him
I showed him from here to there and where
Grief enters and escapes from my hands
In many stanzas and verses or prose
Languages, where I have been muffled
By grief and never had the chance to live
How do the arts of poetry bring you life
Because all I behold before poetry is death

**Another way to go into extinction**

And when I die
In this battle,
They returned
With the sad news.
They told my tales,
About the unknown,
This is a picture of
An unknown black negro -
Who fought alongside
Of the queen's men.

# AUTHOR BIO

**John Chinaka Onyeche** is an author, poet, and teacher of History and African History. He is the author of *Echoes Across The Atlantic*, *A Night Tale At The Threshold Of Howl*, *We Returned To Kiss The Cross*, *The Broken Fort*, *A Good Day For Tomorrow's Coming*, *Stateless*, *21 Atonements*, and a chapbook *Chapters Of Broken Tales*. He is a Best of Net Nominee. A husband, father and poet from Nigeria. John composes his work from the city of Port Harcourt Rivers State, Nigeria. He is currently a student of History and Diplomatic Studies at Ignatius Ajuru University of Education Port Harcourt Rivers State. When John is not writing, he loves reading.

John Chinaka can be reached through the following means:
Rememberajc.wordpress.com
Facebook.com/jehovahisgood
Twitter.com/apostlejohnchin
Apostlejohnchinaka@gmail.com
https://linktr.ee/Rememberajc
https://internationalbookworld.webador.com/john-chinaka-onyeche

www.ingramcontent.com/pod-product-compliance
Lightning Source LLC
LaVergne TN
LVHW041046150826
845672LV00001B/488

* 9 7 8 2 4 8 7 0 1 7 0 6 1 *